Joseph H. Tritton

Catalogue of a collection of books on gems formed by Joseph H. Tritton

Joseph H. Tritton

Catalogue of a collection of books on gems formed by Joseph H. Tritton

ISBN/EAN: 9783743322028

Manufactured in Europe, USA, Canada, Australia, Japa

Cover: Foto ©Thomas Meinert / pixelio.de

Manufactured and distributed by brebook publishing software
(www.brebook.com)

Joseph H. Tritton

Catalogue of a collection of books on gems formed by Joseph H. Tritton

CATALOGUE

OF A

COLLECTION

OF

BOOKS ON GEMS

FORMED BY

JOSEPH H. TRITTON.

This Catalogue was made

in 1898.

Agostini (Leonardo) Le Gemme Antiche Figurate.

2 vols. Roma, 1686. 4°

America (North). Gems and Precious Stones of [see] Kunz (G. F.)

Angelo (Michel) Le Gemme Antiche Figurate di Michel Angelo.

Roma. 1700, 4°

Assyrians The Mysteries of the Assyrians. Translated by T. Taylor [see] Iamblichus

Astle (Thomas) The Origin and Progress of Writing, as well Hieroglyphic as Elementary ... Also some Account of the Origin and Progress of Printing. London, 1876. 4°

Bartolus (Petrus Sanctus) [see] Santi Bartoli. (P.)

Beger (L.) Thesaurus Brandenburgicus selectus sive Gemmarum et Numismatum Graecorum in Cimeliarchio Electorali Brandenburgico.

     3 vols   Coloniae, Regia 1701. fol.

—————— —— Thesaurus ex Thesauro Palatino selectus sive Gemmarum et Numismatum.

         Heidelbergae, 1685. folio.

[With the Card of Jessy's Bookplate]

Bell (John) Bell's New Pantheon; or Historical Dictionary of the Gods, Demi Gods, Heroes, and Fabulous Personages of Antiquity etc.

2 vols [in 1] London, 1790. 4°

Bessborough Catalogue des Pierres Gravées, tant en relief qu'en Creux de Mylord Comte de Bessborough, dressé par Laurent Natter London, 1761. 4°

Bezold (C.) [Editor] The Tell el-Amarna Tablets in the British Museum, with Auto-type Facsimiles. [Edited by C. Bezold, with an Introduction and Summary by C. Bezold and C. A. T. W. Budge, and a Bibliography.] London, 1892. 4°

Boyle (Robert) An Essay about the Origins
and Virtue of Gems. wherein are propos'd
and Historically illustrated some Conject-
-ures about the Consistence of the matter
of Precious Stones.

London, 1672, 8°.

Bracci (D A) Memorie degli Antichi
Incisori che Scolpirono i Loro Nomi in
Gemme e Cammei con molti Monumenti
Inediti di Antichita Statue Bassirilievi
Gemme.

2 vols   Firenze, 1784, fol,

British Museum   Catalogue of Engraved

Gems in the Department of Greek and

Roman Antiquities

London, 1888, 8°

——————   ——————   The Tell el Amarna Tablets

[see]   Bezold (C.)

Cabinet de Pierres Antiques Gravées ou Collection Choisie de 216 Bagues et de 682 Pierres tirées du Cabinet de Gorlée et autres célèbres Cabinets de L'Europe. 2vols.   Paris, 1778. 4°

Cabiri.   A Dissertation on the Mysteries of the Cabiri.   /sc/   Faber (G.S.)

Castellani (Augusto)   Gems: Notes and Extracts translated from the Italian by Mrs. John Brogden
                          London, 1871. 8°

Chaldeans.   The Mysteries of the Chaldeans, Translated from the Greek by T. Taylor /sc/ Iamblichus

Collection of Engravings of Busts, Gems, etc.
(~)
folio

Cortona Museum. /or/ Museum Cortonense.

Cuperus (Gisbertus) G. Cuperi... Harpocrates,
sive explicatio imagunculae argenteae per-
-antiquae quae in figuram Harpocratis
formata representat solem ejusdem Monu-
-menta Antiqua accedit Stephani de Moine
epistola de Melanophoris.
    Trajecti ad Rhenum apud Franciscum
Halma,   1687, in. 4°

Du Moulinet (Claude) Le Cabinet de la
    Bibliothèque de Sainte Geneviève, conte-
    -nant les Antiquités de la Religion
    des Chrétiens, des Égyptiens, et des
    Romains, etc.
                                Paris, 1692, fol.

Dupuis (Charles François) Abrégé de l'Origine
    de Tous les Cultes ... Quatrième édition,
    ornée du portrait de l'auteur, et aug-
    -mentée etc.
                                Paris, 1822, 12°

Ebermayer (J. M.) Capita Deorum et Illus-
trium Hominum Pacis Bellique Artibus
Clarissimorum nec non Hieroglyphica,
Abraxeæ, et Amuleta quaedam in Gemmis
Francofurti et Lipsiae. 1721. folio

—————— ———— Gemmarum affabre Sculp-
tarum Thesaurus quem suis sumptibus haud
exiguis nec parvo studio Norimbergae, 1720.
Capita Deorum et Illustrium Hominum
Pacis Bellique Artibus Clarissimorum
nec non Hieroglyphica, Abraxeæ, et Amuleta
quaedam in Gemmis
Francofurti et Lipsiae, 1721. folio

Evax. (King of Arabia).   Marbodaei Galli
Caenomensis de Gemmarum lapidumqz pre-
tiosorum formis, naturis atque viribus ...
opusculū ... nūc primū ... cētū forme
versib. locupletatū ... et scholiis ... illus-
tratū p Ulardū Amstelredamū, cujus
studio additæ sunt et praecipuae gemmæ
lapidūqz ptiosoℝ explicatiōes ... Cū scholiis
Pictorii Villingen. [According to the Introduction this work was compiled from a treatise
written by Evax, but it was really composed by
Marbodaeus]   Coloniae.   1539, 8°
Stamped leather Binding.

(†)

Faber (G. S.)   A Dissertation on the Mysteries of the Cabiri; or Great Gods of
Samothrace, Egypt, Troas, Greece, Italy,
and Crete.

     2 vols.   Oxford, 1803, 8°

——— ———   The Origin of Pagan Idolatry
ascertained from Historical Testimony and
Circumstantial Evidence.

     3 vols.   London, 1816, 4°

Ficoronii (Francisci)   Gemmae Antiquae
Litteratae aliaeque rariores accesserunt.
Vetera Monumenta, adnotationibus et
Declarationibus illustrata a P. Nicolao
Galeotti.   .   Romae, 1757, 4°

Galeotti (Niccolò) Museum Odescalchum,
sive Thesaurus Antiquarum gemmarum
quae a Christina Suecorum regina
collectae in Museo Odescalcho adservantur,
et a P. Sancto Bartolo quondam incisae,
nunc primum in lucem proferuntur.
Accesserunt nova deorum ac diarum
idola ... quibus omnibus explanationes
una cum indicibus adjectae sunt

    2 tom.   Romae, 1751 '52. fol

Galerie de Florence et du Palais Pitti. Tab-
leaux Statues, Bas Reliefs, et Camées
dessinés par Wicar avec les explications
par Mongez

    11 vols.   Paris, 1789 1841. fol

Glass   Catalogue of the Collection of Glass formed by Felix Slade Esqr. with Notes on the History of Glass making by Alexander Nesbitt.

Printed for Private Distribution.   1871, 4°

Gorius (A. F.)   Gemmae Antiquae ex Thesauro Mediceo et Privatorum Dactyliothecis Florentiae exhibentes Tabulis Imagines Virorum Illustrium et Deorum.

2 vols.   Florentiae, 1731, fol

———— ————   Thesaurus Gemmarum Antiquarum Astriferarum quae e Compluribus Dactyliothecis Selectae.

3 vols   Florentiae, 1750, fol.

Grace Family. One Hundred and Eight Engravings from Antique Gems in the Possession of Various Collectors. The Plates were Formerly the Property of the Grace Family but now belong to James Vallentin, Sheen Lodge, Walthamstow.

1863, 4°

Grace (Sheffield) Antique Gems in the possession of Sheffield Grace [see] Worlidge (T.)

Gravelles (Levesque de) Recueil de Pierres Gravées Antiques, dessinées, gravées et expliquées   Paris, 1732, 4°

Greville (Hon. C. J.) A Collection of Fifty
Prints from Antique Gems in the Collection
of the Hon. C. J. Greville /see/ Spilsbury (J.)

Greville (Hon. C. J.) Ancient Gems.
/see/ Percy (Earl)

Gronovius (Jacobo) Thesaurus Graecarum Anti-
quitatum in quo continentur Effigies Virorum ac Foeminarum Illustrium, quibus
in Graecis aut Latinis monumentis aliqua
memoriae pars datur et in quocunque
orbis Terrarum spatio ob Historiam.
Volumen Primum. Venetiis, 1732, fol

Iamblichus on the Mysteries of the Egyptians,
Chaldeans, and Assyrians. Translated
from the Greek by Thomas Taylor

London, 1895, 8°

Idolatry. (Pagan) The Origin of Pagan Idol
-atry. / see / Faber (G. S.)

——————— Antique Gems and Rings

2 vols.   London, 1872. 8°

——————— Catalogue of Colonel Leake's Engraved Gems in the Fitzwilliam Museum, with Engravings of the Principal Gems

                              Cambridge. 1870. 4°

——————— Early Christian Numismatics and other Antiquarian Tracts.

                              London, 1873. 8°

——————— ———— The Natural History, Ancient
and Modern, of Precious Stones and Gems
+) and of Precious Metals.
London, 1865, 8°

Kircherus (Athanasius) Oedipus Aegyptiacus
hoc est Universalis Hieroglyphicae Veterum
) 2 vols Romae, 1652, fol.

Knight ( ) Modern and Antique Gems
London, 1828, 8°

Kunz (G. F.) Gems and Famous Stones of
North America. A Popular Description of
their Occurrence, Value, History, Archae-
logy, and of the Collections in which they
exist. New York, 1890, 8°

Lane Poole (Stanley). /see/ Poole (S. Lane).

Leake (Colonel) Catalogue of Colonel Leake's
Engraved Gems in the Fitzwilliam Mus-
eum. By C. W. King.
Cambridge, 1870, 4°

Leonardus (Camillus) The Mirror of Stones;
in which the Nature, Generation, Properties,
Virtues, and various Species of more than
200 different jewels are distinctly described
extracted from the Works of Aristotle,
Pliny, Isiodorus, etc Dedicated by
the Author to Caesar Borgia, now first
translated into English

London, 1750, 8°

Le Pois (Antoine) Discours sur les Medail-
les et Gravures Antiques, principalement
Romaines.

Paris, 1579, small 4°

Licetus (F.) Hieroglyphica sive Antiqua Schemata Gemmarum Annularum quar-cita Moralia, Politica, Historica, Medi-ca, Philosophica, et Sublimiora.

Patavii, 1653, folio

Lippert (P. D.) Dactyliothec Das ist Samm-lung geschnittener steine der alten aus denen vornehmsten Museis in Europa zum nützen der Schönen Kunste und Kunstler.

2 vols and Suppt. Leipzig, 1767 '76, 4°

Macarius. Joannis Macarii Canonici Ariensis Abraxas seu Apistopistus quae est Antiquaria de Gemmis Basilidianis Disquisitio, accedit Abraxas Proteus seu multiformis Gemmae Basilidianae Portentiosa Varietas.

Antuerpiae, 1657. 4°

Marbodus (Bishop of Rennes) Marbodaei Galli Caenomanensis &c. 1539. 8° [see] Evax (King of Arabia)

Mariette (P. J.) Traité des Pierres Gravées, 2 vols. Paris. 1750. folio

Marlborough. Choix de Pierres Antiques Gravées du Cabinet du Duc de Marlborough 2 vols London, 1845. folio

Marlborough.   The Marlborough Gems: being a Collection of Works in Cameo and Intaglio formed by George, Third Duke of Marlborough: with Description and an Introduction. By M. H. Nevil Story-Maskelyne

       Privately Printed   1870. 8°

Maskelyne (M. H. Nevil Story) /see/
       Story-Maskelyne (M. H.)

Mayer (Joseph) F. S. A. Catalogue of the Engraved Gems and Rings in the Collection of J. Mayer, F.S.A. By C. T. Gatty
          London, 1879. 4°

Mead (R.) Museum Meadianum, sive Cata-
logus Nummorum veteris aevi Monument-
orum ac Gemmarum cum aliis quibus-
dam artis recentioris et Naturae Operi-
bus   Londini,   no date, 8°

Middleton (J. Henry) The Engraved Gems
of Classical Times, with a Catalogue of
the Gems in the Fitzwilliam Museum.
                         Cambridge,   1891, 8°

———————— ————   The Lewis Collection
of Gems and Rings in the Possession
of Corpus Christi College, Cambridge,
with an Introductory Essay on Ancient
Gems.
                         London,   1892, 8°

Museum Cortonense in quo vetera Monumenta comprehenduntur Anaglypha, Thoreumata, Gemmae. Inscalpta que quae in Academia Etrusca.   Romae, 1750, folio

Museum Meadianum /or/ Mead (K.)

Museum Odescalchum, sive Thesaurus Antiquarum Gemmarum etc.   1751-'52, folio
             /sic/   Galvotti (N)

shell (Alexander) History of Glass Making.
[ ] Slade (John) Catalogue of
the Collection of Glass etc.

Nicols (Thomas) A Lapidary : or the History
of Precious Stones : with cautions for the
undeceiving of all those that deal with
Precious Stones.
                    Cambridge, 1652, small.

Ogle (George) Gemmae Antiquae Caelatae:
or, a Collection of Gems relating to the
Customs and Habits of the Ancients taken
from the Classics, engraved by C. Du Bose
London, 1741, 4°

Orleans Description des Principales
Pierres Gravées du Cabinet de Monseig-
neur Le Duc d'Orleans
2 vols Paris, 1780, fol.

2

————— ———— Ancient Gems from the Collections of Lord Percy, Hon. C. S. Greville, T. M. Slade. Fifty Plates.

London (published by J. Boydell), no date, 8°

Stosch (Bernard) Pierres Antiques Gravées tirées des Principaux Cabinets de l'Europe. Expliquées par Philippe de Stosch.

(Two Copies). Amsterdam, 1724, folio.

Poniatowski (Prince) Explanatory Catalogue of the Proof Impressions of the Antique Gems possessed by Prince Poniatowski, and now in the Possession of John Tyrrell Esq. By James Prendeville.

London, 1841. 4º

———————— ———————— Photographic Facsimiles of the Antique Gems formerly possessed by Prince Poniatowski. [see] Prendeville (J.)

Poole (Stanley Lane) [Editor] Coins and Medals their Place in History and Art. By the Authors of the British Museum Official Catalogues

Preissler (J.J.) + (S)   A Series of One Hundred
and Ninety eight Original Drawings con-
-sisting of Busts, Gems, Masks, etc. with
Two Portraits of the Artists.

[circa 1730]. folio

With Sir John Rawton's Bookplate.

Prendeville (James) Explanatory Catalogue of
the Proof Impressions of the Antique Gems
possessed by the late Prince Poniatowski
and now in the Possession of John Tyrrell Esq.

London, 1841, 8°

—————— —————— Photographic Facsimiles of
the Antique Gems formerly possessed by the
late Prince Poniatowski, accompanied by a
Description and Poetical Illustrations of each
subject ... together with an Essay on Ancient
Gems and Gem Engraving.

2 vols.   London, 1859. 8°

Recueil d'Antiquités Egyptiennes, Etrusques,
   Grecques, et Romaines.
                     7 vols   Paris, 1761-67, 4°

Roman Antiquities, from Vases, Gems. etc.
              [see]   Moses (x . . .)

——— ——— ——— Raccolta di Came
e Gemme Antiche disegnate da suoi
Originali ed intagliate da Pietro Sante
Bartoli date ora in luce da Francesco
Bartoli.   Roma, 1727, folio

Schlichtegroll (Frédéric) Choix des Principales
Pierres Gravées de la Collection qui appar-
-tenait autrefois au Baron de Stosch et
qui se trouve maintenant dans le Cabinets
du Roi de Prusse, accompagnés des
notes et explications.
        Premier volume.
              Nuremberg,   1798, folio.

Slade (Felix) Catalogue of the Collection of Glass formed by Felix Slade Esq., with Notes on the History of Glass Making by Alexander Nesbitt.

Printed for Private Distribution 1871. 4°

Slade (J. M.) Ancient Gems

[xxv] Percy (Earl)

——————— ——————— A Collection of Fifty Prints from Antique Gems in the Collection of J. M. Slade [xx] Spilsbury (John)

Spilsbury (John) A Collection of Fifty Prints from Antique Gems in the Collections of Earl Percy, the Honourable C. F. Greville, and J. M. Slade Esq.

London, no date, 4°

Story-Maskelyne (M. H. Nevil) The Marlborough Gems, being a Collection of Works in Cameo and Intaglio formed by George, Third Duke of Marlborough: with Descriptions and an introduction.

Privately Printed. 1870, 8°

Streeter (Edwin W) Precious Stones and Gems, their History and Distinguishing Characteristics

London, 1884, 8°

Tassie (James) A Descriptive Catalogue of a
General Collection of Ancient and Modern
engraved Gems, Cameos as well as Intag-
+) lios, taken from the most Celebrated
Cabinets in Europe ... arranged and described
by R. E. Raspe, and Illustrated with Copper-
plates.

      2 vols.   London, 1791, 4°

———— ——— and (William) A Biographical
*) and Critical Sketch, with a Catalogue
of their Portrait Medallions of Modern
Personages.   By John M. Gray.
              Edinburgh, 1894, 8°

Trésor de Numismatique et de Glyptique ou Recueil Général de Médailles, Monnaies, Pierres Gravées, Bas Reliefs, etc. tant anciens que modernes. Iconographie des Empereurs Romains et de leurs Familles.

Paris, 1843. folio X

Tyrrell (John) Catalogue of Antique Gems possessed by Prince Poniatowski. [see] Prendeville (James)

Vallentin (James) One Hundred and Eight
Engravings from Antique Gems in the
Possession of Various Collectors. The Plates
were formerly the Property of the Grace
Family, but now belong to James Vallen-
-tin, Shern Lodge, Walthamstow.

1863, 4°

Vico (Enea) Ex Gemmis et Cameis
antiquorum aliquot monumenta, ab Æ.V.
... incis ... D. Panarolo ... J. J. de Rubeis, B.B.
G.G. Rossi: Roma. [1650?]. 4°
(84 numbered plates, including title.)

Wilde (Jacobus de) Gemmae Selectae Anti-
    quae e Museo Jacobi de Wilde, sive
    Tabulae diis deabusque Gentilium Ornatae,
    per Possessorem Conjecturis, Veterumque
    Poetarum Carminibus Illustratae.
                        Amstelaedamie,   1703, 4°

Winckelmann (Giovanni) Monumenti An-
    tichi Inediti spiegati ed illustrati.
             2 vols   Romae, 1767, folio
        (With the Earl of Aylesford's Bookplate.)

Worlidge (T.) Antique Gems in the Possession of
    Sheffield Grace, etched on copperplates by T.
    Worlidge   London, 1823, 11°

Worlidge (T.) A Select Collection of
    Drawings from Curious Antique Gems:
    most of them in the Possession of the
    Nobility and Gentry of this Kingdom:
  †) etched after the manner of Rembrandt.
                        London, 1768, 4°.

Writing,   The Origin and Progress of Writing.
            [see] Astle (Thomas).

www.ingramcontent.com/pod-product-compliance
Lightning Source LLC
Chambersburg PA
CBHW021535270326
41930CB00008B/1259